Original title:

Inkblot Emotions

Copyright © 2024 Creative Arts Management OÜ

All rights reserved.

Author: Dorian Ashford

ISBN HARDBACK: 978-9916-90-660-6

ISBN PAPERBACK: 978-9916-90-661-3

Rivers of Reflection

In quiet streams, thoughts do flow,
Mirrored skies, a gentle glow.
Ripples dance with secrets untold,
In the depths, stories unfold.

Waves of wisdom brush the shore,
With every ebb, we seek for more.
Currents whisper of days gone by,
In the water, dreams learn to fly.

Whispers in Dark Ink

In shadows deep, secrets align,
Written softly, like fine wine.
Letters formed in twilight's breath,
Crafting tales of life and death.

Each stroke sings a silent tune,
Underneath the watchful moon.
Pages turn with cautious grace,
In the dark, we find our place.

Hues of the Hidden

Colors blend in twilight's embrace,
Shades of dreams, in a quiet space.
Crimson hopes and sapphire fears,
Brush the canvas of our years.

With every stroke, a story we weave,
In the palette of those who believe.
Tints of laughter, shadows of pain,
A masterpiece born from joy and rain.

Beneath Ink and Paper

Underneath the words we write,
Lies a world, hidden from sight.
Stories linger in every fold,
Waiting for voices to be bold.

Ink bleeds dreams upon the page,
A silent roar, a quiet rage.
Each paper whisper, a breath of truth,
Holding the echoes of our youth.

The Fluidity of Forgotten Echoes

Whispers drift through silver night,
Memories fade like distant light.
Shadows dance on silent ground,
In the void, lost dreams are found.

Ghostly tales in twilight speak,
Time weaves tales, both strong and weak.
Fleeting moments stitched in air,
Carried softly, thoughts laid bare.

The Art of Unraveled Dreams

Canvas torn, colors collide,
Visions wander, hearts confide.
Threads of hope, fragile and thin,
In the chaos, light begins.

Each stroke whispers secret tales,
Navigating through stormy gales.
Fragments shimmer, beckoning bright,
Illuminating the dark of night.

Shadows of Unquenchable Thirst

There beneath the burning sky,
Echoes of thirst, a silent cry.
Parched desires stretch and weave,
In the silence, hearts believe.

Waves of longing crash and break,
Every ripple, a chance to wake.
In shadows dark, a spark ignites,
Illuminating endless nights.

Flecks of Hope in Despair

In shadows deep, a light still gleams,
Flecks of hope amidst our dreams.
Fractured spirits, still they rise,
Chasing whispers, seeking skies.

Through the struggle, softly hum,
Beauty blossoms from the numb.
In every heart, a flicker burns,
And from the dark, the wisdom learns.

Splotches of Truth

In colors bright, the truths unfold,
Splotches dance on paper bold.
Each hue a tale, a life, a dream,
In chaos, order finds its gleam.

Splashes whisper secrets deep,
Where silence lay, the colors leap.
The strokes reveal what hearts conceal,
In vibrant forms, the void can heal.

Each mark a shout, a muted scream,
Fragments of hope in torn seams.
In every blot, a story sprawls,
In messy art, the spirit calls.

Beneath the Surface

In depths uncharted, shadows play,
Beneath the waves, the whispers sway.
What lies beneath, a world unseen,
As secrets weave through currents keen.

Threads of light on ripples dance,
Inviting thoughts to take a chance.
The surface calm, a mask applied,
Yet deeper truths cannot be denied.

In tranquil depths, reflections stir,
The heart's desires, a gentle blur.
Beneath the surface, currents swell,
In silent depths, our stories dwell.

Ink Streams of Consciousness

Ink flows freely, thoughts ablaze,
A river winding through the maze.
Each drop a dream, each curve a thought,
In liquid lines, our fancies caught.

Words spill out in a hurried race,
Chasing time, we find our place.
Conscious streams like waters swirl,
In silent chaos, ideas unfurl.

With every stroke, the mind takes flight,
Unraveled truths find wings of light.
In ink's embrace, we dive within,
Through winding paths, the tale begins.

Shadows in the Scribble

In tangled lines, shadows creep,
Within the scribbles, secrets seep.
Figures dance in random play,
Whispers of night, dreams gone astray.

Every curve a story spun,
In hints of light, the shadows run.
Tracing thoughts in messy forms,
Between the lines, the heart transforms.

The scribble holds a silent scream,
A refuge found in chaos' gleam.
Within the shadows, truths may lie,
In scribbled dreams, we learn to fly.

Mysterious Patterns of the Heart

In shadows deep where silence dwells,
A heartbeat whispers secret spells,
Each pulse a story, veiled and rare,
Mysterious patterns woven there.

The rhythm dances, soft and free,
Like autumn leaves on a restless sea,
Echoes of love, both lost and found,
In tender beats that swirl around.

A fleeting glance, a stolen sigh,
The weight of dreams that float and fly,
With every thump, a tale revealed,
In the heart's chamber, truth concealed.

So linger here, let time stand still,
In shadows deep, the heart can thrill,
Embrace the chaos, feel the art,
Of mysterious patterns in the heart.

A Tapestry of Unshed Tears

Threads of sorrow, finely spun,
In daylight's warmth, they come undone,
Each drop a stitch that tells a tale,
Of dreams that flounder, hopes that fail.

Silken strands in softest hues,
Woven moments, bittersweet hues,
A tapestry, both rich and frail,
Of unshed tears and quiet wail.

In corners dark where shadows creep,
Memories linger, secrets keep,
With every tear, a knot is tied,
In this fabric, we confide.

Yet, in the weave, a strength appears,
A story bright amidst the fears,
For through the tears, the light breaks clear,
A tapestry of love, sincere.

The Poetry of Chaos

In tangled webs of frantic thought,
Where order falters, battles fought,
Each word a spark, ignites the night,
The poetry of chaos takes flight.

Raging storms in stormy skies,
A symphony of wild cries,
Yet in this turmoil, beauty gleams,
Dancing shadows, shattered dreams.

Fragments flutter, lost and free,
In madness lies the key to see,
A disarray that speaks so true,
The poetry of chaos shines through.

So let it swirl, this vibrant dance,
A whirlwind of fate, a wild chance,
For in the chaos, hearts unite,
Creating art in endless flight.

Tangled Lines of Longing

In twilight's hush, where shadows blend,
A yearning heart begins to mend,
Tangled lines of what we seek,
In whispers soft, our spirits speak.

Each moment stretched, a fragile thread,
In every sigh, a word unsaid,
Longing folds into the night,
Wishing on stars that burn so bright.

Yet in this maze of love and fear,
We find a path that feels so near,
With every twist, a chance to grow,
In tangled lines, our longings flow.

So paint the dawn with hopes anew,
In gentle strokes of love so true,
For tangled lines, they comfort still,
In longing hearts, a boundless thrill.

Fluid Scars

In the river of time, we flow,
Carrying shadows of what we know.
Each ripple holds a silent plea,
Wounds that linger, yet set free.

Beneath the surface, scars will lie,
Whispers of battles fought and shy.
The current erodes, but we remain,
Healing hearts wrapped in the pain.

Like waves that kiss the sandy shore,
We embrace each bruise, wanting more.
Fluid memories leak and blend,
A story of loss that will not end.

Yet, in the depths, light starts to gleam,
Through tangled paths, we find our dream.
Fluid scars become our art,
Tales of courage, woven heart.

Mosaics of Mood

Colors dance on a canvas bright,
Each hue a tale in radiant light.
Fragments of laughter, sorrow, delight,
Mosaics of mood, glittering in sight.

Shades of blue whisper of the rain,
While sunny yellows banish the pain.
Greens soothe the spirit, calm and wise,
In every stroke, a story lies.

Crimson streaks of passion ignite,
A fervent heart in the cool of night.
Tangled emotions, raw and true,
Overlapping layers create the view.

From somber grays to vibrant gold,
Each fragment reflects what we behold.
Together they form a life anew,
A mosaic of mood, written for you.

The Silent Crescendo

In whispers soft, the world unfolds,
A symphony of secrets yet untold.
Notes linger in the hush of night,
The silent crescendo takes its flight.

Shadows dance on the edge of sound,
Echoes of dreams that wrap around.
Each heartbeat a rhythm, faint yet clear,
Connecting the moments that we hold dear.

Amidst the quiet, thoughts collide,
Waves of emotion, unable to hide.
The crescendo rises, soft, sublime,
Carving our stories in sacred time.

As silence swells, we start to see,
The beauty lies in what will be.
In the stillness, we find our way,
The silent crescendo leads our play.

Abstract Thoughts Unraveled

Colors blend in chaotic grace,
Thoughts untangle in a vibrant space.
Fractals of reason, wild and free,
Abstract musings floating in the sea.

Each stroke of whimsy shapes the mind,
Curving paths that intertwine.
Reality bends, a playful tease,
In the realm of thought, we find our ease.

A canvas of stars, ideas collide,
Unraveling truths we wish to hide.
Surreal whispers, profound yet light,
In abstract realms, we take our flight.

Through tangled webs, we weave and twine,
A journey through the maze of the divine.
Thoughts unfurl like petals in bloom,
In the abstract, we find our room.

Shadowed Stains of Feelings

In corners deep, where shadows linger,
Emotions twist like knotted string.
Each stain a tale, a heart's soft whisper,
In silence lost, what hearts may bring.

Memories drip in hues of sorrow,
Faded dreams in twilight's grasp.
With every breath, the weight of tomorrow,
And moments gone we try to clasp.

Yet hope ignites a spark within,
As shadows dance in dusk's embrace.
Through darkest nights, new light begins,
To wash away the pain we face.

So let us rise from shadows deep,
And paint our lives with colors bright.
For every stain, a promise keeps,
That love will guide us to the light.

Splotches of Silence

Upon the canvas, colors drip,
Hushed tones of an unspoken plea.
Each stroke a longing, a fleeting slip,
In shades of gray, what's left to see?

The quiet echoes through the air,
As splotches blend in frail delight.
In every pause, a world laid bare,
The heart beats soft, yet full of fright.

Yet silence knows the space of grace,
In gaps where words would often fade.
With every breath, a slower pace,
We find the depth where dreams are laid.

So here we stand, in silent thought,
Amidst the chaos, peace can thrive.
In splotches bright, the battles fought,
Through silence found, our spirits strive.

Whispers in Uncharted Currents

Among the waves where secrets glide,
Whispers travel on the breeze.
In currents deep, where dreams reside,
Life's journey flows with gentle ease.

Each ripple speaks of tales untold,
Of ships that sail through night's embrace.
In depths of blue, a heart of gold,
Navigating paths that time can trace.

With every sway, a truth revealed,
As stars ignite the velvet sky.
The ocean's breath, a fate concealed,
A whispered wish, a love's soft cry.

So let us wander, hand in hand,
Through uncharted depths, we'll find our way.
For in the currents, we can stand,
And face whatever comes our day.

Colors of Conflicted Souls

In vibrant strokes of heart's desire,
Two souls collide, yet dance apart.
A palette rich, with joy and fire,
Yet paints a canvas torn at heart.

One moment bright, the next in shade,
Conflict born from love's embrace.
As colors swirl, decisions made,
Reveal the pain we cannot face.

Yet through the clash, a beauty blooms,
In every hue, a story shared.
Through darkest nights, love still consumes,
Together forged, despite the scared.

Embrace the clash, the push, the pull,
For here we find our truest selves.
Through every shade, both light and dull,
In colors bright, our love compels.

The Weight of Blurred Memories

Soft whispers cling to faded dreams,
Moments lost in the drifting seams.
Footsteps echo, shadows cast,
Time obscures the ties we grasp.

Lingering scents of yesterdays,
Fragrant memories, a sweet haze.
Heavy hearts and tangled threads,
In silence, the past gently spreads.

Faded photos, edges worn,
Stories linger, love poignantly torn.
The weight of the past, a heavy crown,
In the twilight, we wear it down.

Yet amidst the blur, hope persists,
In the chaos, a soft twist.
Memories fade but never stray,
They shape us still in their own way.

Answering the Chaos

In the whirlwind of thoughts that race,
We seek moments, a quiet space.
Voices clash in disarray,
Finding peace in the fray.

Questions float like autumn leaves,
Caught in currents that never grieve.
Each sound is a cue, a call,
Navigating through it all.

Amidst the noise, a gentle sigh,
A whisper soft as the evening sky.
We gather fragments, shape our maze,
Answering chaos in its blaze.

With every tremor, a chance to grow,
In the chaos, let our spirits flow.
Together we stand, strong and clear,
Finding our rhythm, erasing fear.

Emotions Lost in the Mist

Veiled shadows, thoughts entwined,
In the fog, what will we find?
Frayed edges of a vivid thought,
Fragments of feelings, so tightly caught.

Whispers dance in the pale twilight,
Emotions lost, a gradual flight.
Silent echoes of a heart once bold,
Stories buried, waiting to be told.

Distant silhouettes emerge and flee,
In the haze, what's left of me?
Faint glimmers of what we were,
In the mist, our memories stir.

Yet in this haze, we must believe,
Hope lingers, it will not leave.
For even lost in the drifting air,
Emotions linger, everywhere.

The Spectrum of a Broken Heart

A canvas splashed with colors bright,
Each stroke a shade of lost delight.
Crimson tears and shades of blue,
Reflecting pain born from the true.

Streaks of anger, whispers of grief,
In this turmoil, there's no relief.
Yet in the cracks, a spark may bloom,
A fragile flower in shadowed gloom.

Through the hues of heartache, we paint,
A masterpiece, though weary and quaint.
Every hue a tale unspoken,
In the silence, hearts are broken.

But from the pain, we learn to rise,
Crafting hope from bitter sighs.
The spectrum wide, our hearts embrace,
In every shade, we find our place.

Drips and Dribbles

Raindrops tap on window glass,
Whispers of a stormy past.
Each little drip a tale to tell,
Of earth and sky and water's swell.

Puddles form in shaded nooks,
Reflecting dreams like storybooks.
Nature's canvas, wet and wild,
Dancing with joy, a playful child.

In the gardens, blooms now sway,
Cleansed by dribbles of yesterday.
Life awakens with each drop,
As time flows gently, never stops.

Listen closely, hear the sound,
In the drips, light can be found.
Every moment, fleeting grace,
Holds the world in a soft embrace.

Written in the Silence

In the stillness, thoughts take flight,
Crafting words in quiet night.
Pages filled with whispers low,
Stories only silence knows.

The heart converses with the mind,
In gentle shadows, truth we find.
Written softly, lines appear,
Every silence holds a tear.

Moments stretch like endless threads,
Braiding dreams and thoughts unsaid.
Between the beats, the worlds collide,
Where silence breathes, our hopes abide.

In quietude, the soul can dance,
Finding peace in a silent trance.
Every pause, a chance to see,
The beauty in tranquility.

Echoes of the Soul

In the valley, echoes bloom,
Voices linger, dispel the gloom.
Softly calling from afar,
Reminding us who we are.

The mountains hold our whispered fears,
Captured in a thousand years.
Every echo, a story told,
In the silence, dreams unfold.

From deep within, the memories rise,
Reflections found in twilight skies.
Each note a thread, a timeless goal,
Weaving echoes of the soul.

As stars ignite and fade away,
Our hearts listen to what they say.
In the night, a guiding light,
Echoes lead us through the night.

Tides of Turmoil

Underneath the raging sky,
Waves of chaos roll and sigh.
The ocean's breath, a moaning sound,
In its depths, lost dreams are found.

Storms collide with shore's embrace,
Nature's fury, a wild chase.
Each swell a testament of strife,
Telling tales of stormy life.

In the turmoil, hearts may break,
Yet from shadows, light we make.
Rising tides, relentless flow,
Through the struggle, we shall grow.

As calm returns, the waters clear,
Lessons learned, we hold them near.
In the dance of rise and fall,
We find our strength through it all.

Tides of Joy and Grief

The ocean whispers soft and low,
As waves of joy and sorrow flow.
In every crest, a smile or tear,
A dance of hopes, a tinge of fear.

The moonlight drapes the beach in peace,
While tides of grief begin to cease.
Memories rise, like seashells bright,
Holding warmth within the night.

Echoes of laughter fill the air,
Yet shadows linger everywhere.
The ebb and flow, forever entwined,
In currents deep, the heart aligned.

Together they weave a tale profound,
In every heartbeat, love is found.
The tides both calm and tempestuous,
Embrace us all, they guide us thus.

Colors That Speak in Tongues

A canvas laid in hues untold,
Whispers of stories, brave and bold.
Crimson dreams and azure skies,
In every stroke, a world that lies.

Golden sunbeams spill their rays,
Painting the moments of our days.
Emerald shadows dance with grace,
In every shade, we find our place.

Voices of colors blend and sway,
In silent verses, they convey.
A palette rich with tales unseen,
Where every line meets space serene.

In this spectrum, hearts unite,
Finding solace in the light.
Each color whispers, soft, yet strong,
A language deep where we belong.

Shadows on the Page

Ink drips slowly, secrets unfold,
Stories waiting, brave and bold.
Shadows linger, words to share,
In the margins, whispers flare.

Each letter dances, soft and bright,
Casting hints of day and night.
In every paragraph, hope glows,
While darkness in the silence grows.

Characters breathe in ink's embrace,
Living moments, time and space.
The shadows hide what we can't see,
Layers deep, a mystery.

Together they weave a life defined,
In every story, love entwined.
The pages turn, the shadows play,
As dreams and thoughts just drift away.

Fragments of the Heart

Pieces scattered, lost and found,
In every fragment, love profound.
Shattered dreams and whispered lies,
In tender moments, hope still flies.

Hearts are puzzles, torn apart,
But in the cracks, there grows a spark.
Each broken edge tells tales anew,
As time reveals what once we knew.

Memories linger, soft and warm,
In fragments, we find strength, not harm.
With every shard, we piece the whole,
A journey deep within the soul.

Together we mend what once was torn,
In every heart, a love reborn.
Through trials faced, we stand as one,
In fragments, life has just begun.

Dripped Essence of Dreams

In twilight whispers, dreams unfold,
A canvas painted with hues of gold.
Stars twinkle softly, a silent glow,
Guiding lost wishes, where spirits flow.

Shadows dance gently, in soft embrace,
Time drips slow, in this sacred space.
Mirrors reflect what the heart believes,
In the essence of dreams, the soul weaves.

Each drop a story, a fleeting glance,
Moments suspended in a timeless dance.
Awakened visions, both fragile and bright,
Illuminate paths in the velvety night.

With each heartbeat, desires ignite,
The dripped essence finds its light.
In a world of wonder, deep and wide,
Dreams bloom gently, in fate's own stride.

Mismatched Moods on Canvas

Colors collide in chaotic embrace,
Swirls and strokes, a wild chase.
Vibrant reds clash with muted gray,
Each hue speaks what words cannot say.

A splash of blue, a hint of gold,
Emotions captured, both brave and bold.
Shapes of sorrow, lines of delight,
Mismatched moods dance in the light.

Brush in hand, a heart laid bare,
Each stroke reveals, each color shares.
Chaos harmonizes, a puzzling whole,
Reflections of life in every soul.

As layers build, the canvas sighs,
Stories emerge with each muted cry.
In mismatched moods, art finds its way,
Whispers of color, in love's ballet.

Hidden Stories in Every Smudge

In the corners where shadows blend,
Hidden stories begin and end.
A gentle touch leaves traces behind,
Every smudge a story to find.

Fingers linger on faded lines,
Secrets woven, like tangled vines.
Echoes of laughter, whispers of pain,
In quiet corners, the past remains.

A chance encounter, a fleeting glance,
Marks the surface of life's dance.
Each smudge a tale, a memory spun,
Forgotten fragments of what was done.

Through ink and paint, the heart confides,
Hidden stories, where truth resides.
In every blemish, a life embraced,
The raw and real, no moments misplaced.

Fluid Echoes of the Heart

Ripples of feelings, softly collide,
In a vast ocean where passions abide.
Waves carry whispers, gentle yet clear,
Fluid echoes resonate, drawing near.

With every pulse, the tides they turn,
An ebb and flow, a lesson learned.
Hearts like rivers, they wander and drift,
In the depths of love, we find our gift.

The currents of trust shape every bend,
Along this journey, our hearts transcend.
In stillness and storm, we find our way,
Fluid echoes guide us, night and day.

Through quiet reflections, we sense the art,
Of flowing dreams, where the waters start.
In every whisper, a promise flows,
In fluid echoes, the heart always knows.

Resonance in the Mess

Amid the chaos, echoes swell,
Whispers of truths we dare not tell.
Fragments scattered, yet they hum,
A symphony lost, but never numb.

In the clutter, a rhythm grows,
Tangled paths that only few know.
Each note a story, deep and raw,
Resonance found in every flaw.

Seeking clarity through the haze,
Dancing shadows in the rays.
A pause, a breath, a moment made,
In the mess, our hearts cascade.

These echoes form a fragile bond,
A reminder of where we belong.
In disarray, we weave our song,
Resonance in the mess, so strong.

Untamed Sparks of Emotion

Fires ignite with a sudden flare,
Hearts ablaze in the open air.
Untamed feelings, wild and free,
A dance of chaos, just you and me.

In fleeting moments, passions bloom,
Lighting up the darkest room.
Every glance, an electric charge,
In the silence, desires enlarge.

A spark can turn into a blaze,
In the frenzy, we lose our way.
Heartbeats clash in a primal fight,
Untamed sparks tear through the night.

Emotions rise like waves at sea,
Challenging the core of who we be.
Through every storm, we find a way,
Untamed sparks lead our hearts to sway.

The Spectrum of Hidden Battles

Behind closed doors, the struggles hide,
Masquerades worn with practiced pride.
Colors clash in silent war,
The spectrum's depth we can't ignore.

Each hue tells tales, both dark and bright,
Shadows whispering through the night.
In every glance, a story lies,
The battles fought beneath the skies.

Glimmers of hope in the gray despair,
Faint echoes of voices, soft and rare.
Each stroke of pain, a lesson learned,
The canvas of life, by heart, we yearned.

With every wave that crashes hard,
A new dawn rises, bruised but scarred.
In the spectrum, we find our peace,
Hidden battles seek release.

Fleeting Traces of Desire

In autumn's whisper, desires twirl,
Breathless moments in a swirling whirl.
Fleeting glances, soft and light,
The dance of longing ignites the night.

Crimson petals fall like sighs,
Drifting softly, under the skies.
Each fleeting trace a secret shared,
A fleeting glance, a life laid bare.

Memories linger, sweet like wine,
Wishes woven in the design.
In silence, hearts quietly ache,
Fleeting traces that time can't shake.

Chasing shadows in twilight's glow,
Yearning for things we cannot know.
Yet in the fleeting, beauty lies,
Traces of desire, never dies.

Swirling Confusion in Monochrome

In shadows thick, the edges blur,
Thoughts intertwine, a silent stir.
Black and white, a dance of doubt,
In silence loud, the whispers shout.

Fragments lost in twisted views,
Color fades, yet shapes confuse.
A mind adrift on waves of gray,
In blurred lines, I seek the way.

Voices mingled, undefined,
In the fray, clarity maligned.
Chasing dreams wrapped in haze,
In monochrome, I drift and gaze.

Yet in the chaos, light shall break,
A spark to lift the heavy ache.
Amidst the swirl, a truth shall form,
In swirling chaos, strength is born.

Portraits of Unspoken Words

In silence hang the tales untold,
Each glance, a memory, bright yet cold.
The canvas waits, a heart laid bare,
Brush strokes linger, thoughts ensnare.

A portrait speaks in hues of ache,
Unfolding truths that silence makes.
Fingers trace the subtle lines,
Echoes dance where meaning twines.

Whispers trapped in fragile frames,
Capture dreams, ignite the flames.
With every breath, a story grows,
In the quiet, the heart knows.

Colors bleed, emotions flow,
In every shade, the secrets sow.
Framed in quiet, the voices merge,
Portraits speak where words converge.

The Plea of a Blotted Page

Ink runs wild, emotions spill,
Letters lost, a heart to fill.
Each blot a tear, a silent plea,
Yearning for words to set them free.

A paper stained with dreams unseen,
Faded stories, where hope has been.
Lines erased with every drop,
Yet still the ink will never stop.

The whispers trapped in smeared despair,
Caught in a dance, a fragile air.
In blots, a tale of love and loss,
A journey penned, no matter the cost.

Yet through the mess, a spark still glows,
In every stain, a heart that knows.
With blot and smudge, the truth will wage,
A call to life, the blotted page.

Serenity Amidst the Spills

In chaos bright, the spills are spread,
Yet still a calm within the dread.
Where colors mix, and shadows play,
A moment's peace will find its way.

The softest hues, like breath of night,
Wrap 'round the heart, an ethereal light.
Quiet whispers through the noise,
In chaos found, I hear my voice.

Amidst the spills, the journey flows,
Embracing all that nature shows.
A dance of colors, wild and free,
In every drop, serenity.

Through life's spills, a truth shall bloom,
Finding grace within the gloom.
In stormy seas, I've learned to hold,
A calm that shines, a heart of gold.

The Brush of Euphoria

With colors bright and bold,
Joy dances upon the page,
Each stroke a story told,
In this vibrant, fleeting stage.

Whispers of a summer's day,
Where laughter fills the air,
Euphoria leads the way,
In moments pure and rare.

The canvas beams with delight,
A symphony of hues,
Every shade holds a light,
Bringing forth sweet muse.

In the heart of creation,
A joy we can't contain,
Lost in pure sensation,
Euphoria's sweet refrain.

Shades of Lament in the Margins

In margins worn and creased,
Stories linger, soft and gray,
Whispers of the pain released,
Memories that slowly fray.

A tear on crinkled lines,
Ink bleeds through the silent space,
Between the sorrowed signs,
Lament fills the empty trace.

Colors fade like old regrets,
In shadows, dreams do crawl,
These notes, the heart begets,
Shades of loss in silence fall.

Yet hope clings onto the edge,
Like sunlight breaking through,
In every sorrowed pledge,
A flicker can renew.

The Heart's Uncharted Terrain

In valleys deep, where shadows lie,
The heart ventures far and wide,
With every pulse, a silent cry,
In uncharted paths, we confide.

Mountains rise, steep and tall,
Each echo, a distant call,
Through thickets thick and wild,
We wander, lost yet beguiled.

Rivers twist like fateful dreams,
Where emotions ebb and flow,
In the silence, the heart gleams,
Guided by the stars' soft glow.

Exploring what feels unknown,
With courage, we shall roam,
In this journey of our own,
We find the way back home.

Abstract Interpretations of Heartache

Shapes and shadows blend and blur,
Feelings twine like threads of fate,
In this canvas, pain demurs,
Yet beauty lies in every state.

Splashes of a muted hue,
Every stroke, a silent scream,
The heartache pulls me into you,
We float within this fractured dream.

Lines intertwine, both sharp and soft,
Each curve tells a tale of loss,
Yet rising high, we drift aloft,
Finding meaning in the dross.

Through the art of breaking free,
We paint in shades of hope,
In abstract forms, we come to see,
Heartache's path, a wondrous slope.

Chaotic Currents of Acceptance

In the swirl of life's mad race,
We find a calm, a gentle space.
Acceptance flows like a river's tide,
Embracing all that we can't hide.

Waves crash and pull, yet we remain,
Learning to dance through joy and pain.
In currents wild, our hearts still beat,
Finding peace where chaos meets.

Each turn we take, a lesson learned,
In fierce embrace, our spirits yearned.
Ride the waves, both rough and smooth,
In acceptance, we find our groove.

So let the currents take their course,
In every change, we'll find a source.
Trust the tides, let go the fight,
In chaos, we discover light.

The Untold Distance of Hues

Colors whisper secrets bright,
Painting dreams in soft twilight.
An emerald joy, a sapphire sigh,
Where shadows dance, and hopes can fly.

In every shade, a story lies,
A canvas rich beneath the skies.
Crimson sunsets, golden dawns,
Each hue a heartbeat, love reborn.

Violets share their tender grace,
In this vast, uncharted space.
A palette bold, yet calm and true,
The distance fades in shades of blue.

So let us roam through colors wide,
With every hue, we choose a side.
In the spectrum's reach, we feel,
A distant bond, forever real.

Shadows that Whisper

The shadows rest soft on the wall,
In silence, they dance, heed their call.
Whispers of secrets dark and deep,
A world unseen, where echoes creep.

In twilight's embrace, they softly mold,
Stories of warmth, and some of cold.
They linger close, yet drift away,
As twilight fades into the day.

With every step, their secrets stir,
In hushed tones, they silently blur.
A symphony sung in muted light,
Shadows that whisper through the night.

Embrace the dark; it holds the key,
To understand what sets us free.
In every shadow, a tale to tell,
In whispered depths, we know it well.

Fluidity of Uncertainty

Life flows like water, never still,
A river's path bends to its will.
In uncertainty's grasp, we drift along,
Finding strength in a world so strong.

Moments sway like leaves in breeze,
Each shift reminds us, we must seize.
The beauty that lies in what we face,
In fluid dance, we find our place.

Questions rise like vapor in air,
Yet with each breath, we learn to care.
Embrace the unknown, let go of fear,
In this fluidity, we draw near.

So sway with the currents, trust the flow,
In uncertainty's arms, we learn and grow.
With every twist, a chance to see,
The beauty found in being free.

The Canvas of Yearning

In twilight hues of deep desire,
The brushstrokes dance, hearts catch fire.
Each stroke whispers tales untold,
Dreams painted bright, yet still so bold.

Seeking shadows, where hopes reside,
Across the canvas, emotions glide.
With every color, a story flows,
In the silence, the yearning grows.

A palette mixed with fear and grace,
In each corner, a familiar face.
As colors merge and borders fade,
The inner world of dreams is laid.

Now stands a piece, a living truth,
A blend of sorrow, joy, and youth.
In every layer, passion sings,
A canvas born of hidden things.

Scribbles of Serenity

In gentle swirls of softest ink,
Peace spills over, inviting to think.
The page, a refuge for the mind,
Where chaos pauses, calm we find.

Lines that curve with tender grace,
Each scribble leaves a warm embrace.
In quiet moments, thoughts unwind,
A tranquil heart learns to be kind.

Every loop a sigh of relief,
In simple marks, we find belief.
Beneath the surface, still waters flow,
As worlds emerge in quiet glow.

With every doodle, stories weave,
A tapestry that weaves and cleaves.
In scribbles small, find serenity,
A dance of peace, pure and free.

More Than Black and White

In the monochrome of life we tread,
Yet colors beckon, visions spread.
Beyond the gray, where dreams ignite,
Shadows whisper of inner light.

A palette rich, of hues unseen,
In every gray, a glow might gleam.
For every shade that paints the soul,
A vibrant truth makes us whole.

Life's not a sketch, so blunt, so stark,
In nuance lies the hidden spark.
As brush meets canvas, so we strive,
To find the shades that make us thrive.

From black and white, a rainbow grows,
In every heart, a universe glows.
Beyond the stark, let colors dance,
In vivid dreams, we find our chance.

Patterns of the Unseen

In whispers soft, the patterns play,
A dance of threads, both night and day.
Woven secrets in every seam,
Where silent echoes weave a dream.

Beneath the surface, forms align,
A tapestry of fate, divine.
Each knot and twist, a path unfolds,
The beauty lies in what's not told.

Hidden rhythms, hearts entwined,
In sacred space, our souls combined.
As threads connect and shadows fade,
In intricate designs, we're made.

Look closer still, see what lies bare,
In patterns thick, love fills the air.
For in the unseen, life's tales unfold,
A rich mosaic of hearts, bold.

Fluid Whispers of the Mind

Thoughts drift like gentle streams,
Carrying secrets, untold dreams.
In shadows where silence plays,
A labyrinth of silent rays.

Echoes of laughter, faint and low,
Wander through the ebb and flow.
Fragments of time, lost and found,
In the whispers that resound.

Mirages dance in twilight's embrace,
Fleeting glimmers of a place.
Thoughts intertwine, soft and light,
In the stillness of the night.

A canvas of shades in quiet hues,
Painting feelings, subtle clues.
Fluid whispers, ever so free,
Guide the heart to what can be.

Stains of Solitude

In corners dark, shadows creep,
Where silence dwells and memories seep.
Time lingers heavy, lost in thought,
In the solitude that life has brought.

Like ink that bleeds on paper's edge,
A mark of knowing, a silent pledge.
Each heartbeat echoes, faint yet clear,
In the stained corners, I face my fear.

Views from windows, fogged and gray,
Reveal the world that slips away.
Loneliness wraps, a shroud so tight,
In the depths of long, forsaken nights.

Yet in the stillness, strength is born,
From weary hearts that feel the scorn.
With every stain, a tale to tell,
In solitude, I learn to dwell.

Veils of Ink

With every stroke, a tale unfolds,
Emotions wrapped in stories told.
Ink drips softly, like falling rain,
Whispers of joy, echoes of pain.

Veils of color, soft and deep,
In the silence where dreams sleep.
Pages turn, a dance of light,
Illuminating dark with insight.

Ink flows freely, a river wide,
Carrying secrets we cannot hide.
In shadows long, we find our peace,
As the heart's burden starts to cease.

Artistry born from the inkwell's might,
Crafted in the quiet of night.
Veils of ink, forever bound,
In the silence, beauty is found.

The Spectrum of Feelings

Colors blend in vibrant hues,
Unfolding stories, old and new.
From violet calm to fiery red,
A spectrum dances, feelings spread.

Joy erupts in bursts of light,
While sorrow dims the day to night.
Each color whispers, soft yet loud,
Woven within a silent crowd.

Tender greens of hope arise,
Soft blues that calm the restless skies.
In every shade, a truth set free,
Reflecting all that's meant to be.

The spectrum pulses, a living art,
Each feeling holds a piece of heart.
In every moment, raw and real,
Life's canvas paints the way we feel.

Calligraphy of Ambivalence

In twisted strokes, the ink does flow,
Between the lines, uncertainty glows.
Hearts that flutter, yet stand still,
In every choice, the quiet thrill.

A page divides the truth and lie,
With every swirl, a silent cry.
The pen, a wand of heated dreams,
Writes down hopes in tangled schemes.

In shadows deep, intentions clash,
A lingering doubt, a sudden flash.
The script unfolds, then slips away,
Caught in the dance of bright and gray.

In every curve, a story's weight,
A lover's pen that seals their fate.
Ambivalence held beneath the skin,
A calligrapher's secret sin.

The Weight of Unfurling Shadows

As twilight bends, the shadows creep,
While secrets in their silence sleep.
The weight of dusk, a heavy shroud,
In every breath, whispers loud.

Branches bend, but never break,
In nature's hush, a world awake.
The looming night brings tales untold,
In echoes soft, the dark unfolds.

Each fleeting moment, shadows blend,
The line of day, where colors bend.
In every corner, mystery thrives,
A heavy heart, where silence survives.

Yet in that weight, there lies a spark,
A ghostly glow that lights the dark.
In unfurling grace, we find our way,
Through night's embrace, to break of day.

A Dance of Color and Gloom

In vibrant strokes, the canvas sighs,
With hues that whisper, beneath the skies.
A dance begins, where light does gleam,
Yet shadows linger, like a dream.

Splashes bright against the gray,
Moments lost in disarray.
The brush, a wand of vast extremes,
Paints out laughter, alongside screams.

In every corner, tales collide,
Where joy and sorrow, side by side.
A watercolor heart, all torn apart,
Yet finds its way to be a part.

Celebrate the light, welcome the night,
In this dance, both bold and slight.
For in the blend, we see the truth,
A tapestry of living youth.

The Language of Smeared Sentiments

Ink runs wild upon the page,
Emotions spill, a silent rage.
Words catch fire, then fade to dust,
In smeared lines, we place our trust.

Unspoken thoughts, a tender mess,
A heart that aches, seeks to confess.
The language formed by hands that shake,
In every smear, a chance to break.

Each letter bends, distorts, then flows,
A story hidden, still it grows.
In chaos bright, we find our sound,
In smeared sentiments, love is found.

So let the ink run free tonight,
Embrace the flaws, embrace the fight.
In every mark, a truth untamed,
In language smeared, our hearts reclaimed.

Merging Hues of Discontent

Shadows dance with fleeting light,
A canvas smeared with muted fright.
Colors clash in a silent scream,
Fractured edges, a broken dream.

Whispers echo through the night,
Promises lost, out of sight.
Each stroke tells a tale of woe,
In the blend, emotions flow.

Rusty reds and dulling greens,
Paint the truth beneath the scenes.
Yet through the chaos, hope does gleam,
A flicker born from despair's seam.

Merging hues, a portrait bleak,
Words unspoken, hearts still seek.
In the mess, we find our plea,
To rise anew, to simply be.

Fractured Reflections of the Mind

Mirrors crack, the image splits,
Thoughts collide, and reason flits.
Fleeting echoes of the past,
In shards of glass, we hold them fast.

Conversations haunt the empty space,
Each reflection, a different face.
In chaos, clarity is sought,
Yet in this war, are we all caught?

In the labyrinth of what we feel,
Answers hidden, none reveal.
Pieces scattered, yet they bind,
Fractured paths of the weary mind.

Truths glimpsed through jagged seams,
Life unwinds in shattered dreams.
Yet hope remains within the shards,
A light to guide, though the path is hard.

Detours in Ink

Ink spills over the empty page,
A journey starts, unmarked by age.
Each line drawn, a step away,
From certainty, into the fray.

Words meander like rivers wide,
Taking turns, they often hide.
In the detours, wisdom flows,
Through winding paths, the spirit grows.

Exploration in every stroke,
A tale unfolding, a quiet joke.
With every pivot, a chance to learn,
In ink's embrace, bright passions burn.

The map is drawn with hearts and mind,
In detours, the treasures we find.
Through each sidestep, we redefine,
The beauty found in verses' line.

The Abyss of Unwritten Thoughts

An empty page, a haunting tale,
Whispers linger, yet I pale.
Inkless dreams in shadows rest,
Yearning deep within my chest.

What words remain, locked away?
Forbidden echoes, lost in gray.
The silence stretches far and wide,
An abyss where feelings hide.

Visions dance just out of sight,
Fleeting glimpses of pure light.
Yet the pen remains still in hand,
As I grapple with the unplanned.

In this void, I seek to dive,
To catch the sparks and keep them alive.
But the abyss calls, cold and vast,
Each unwritten thought, a shadow cast.

The Palette of Ghostly Memories

In shadows cast by fading light,
The whispers of the past take flight.
Fleeting visions dance and swoon,
A tapestry of dreams in June.

Colors bleed on canvas rare,
Sculpting tales of love and care.
Each brushstroke glimmers with a sigh,
Echoes of the days gone by.

Fractal paths of joy and pain,
Trace the lines of loss and gain.
In silence, all the moments weave,
A haunted art that won't deceive.

Yet in the canvas, hope survives,
Through ghostly hues, the spirit thrives.
For every shade of grief and glee,
The heart remembers how to be.

Doodles of Dismay

On crumpled pages, scribbles lay,
Words once bright now fade to gray.
Fleeting thoughts in haste undone,
Trapped in lines where dreams have run.

The ink runs dry; the mood distorts,
With tangled sketches, solace courts.
A frown too deep, a smile too faint,
In every mark, a voice grows quaint.

Beneath the chaos, a flicker glows,
A tale of struggle, the heart bestows.
Within the doodles, truth unfolds,
A map of feelings too bold to hold.

Yet from the dismay, a spark takes flight,
Creativity birthed from the night.
With every line, the shadows sway,
In the art of chaos, find your way.

Arcane Symbols of Fragile Hearts

In whispers soft, the symbols lie,
Guarding secrets none can pry.
A language drawn in scars and tears,
Speaking truths beyond the years.

Circles, lines entwined with grace,
Mapping paths where lovers place.
Through fragments lost, the heart reveals,
The hidden weight of all it feels.

Patterns carved on paper thin,
Crafting tales of where we've been.
Each arcane sign, a piece of fate,
Fractured souls that resonate.

Yet in each stroke, resilience shows,
Through fragile hearts, true love still grows.
These symbols guide, though they may part,
A sacred bond within the heart.

Resilience of An Unwritten Poem

On pages blank, the whispers call,
A silent strength that conquers all.
With every pause, a heartbeat sings,
The weight of dreams, the joy it brings.

In every line that hesitates,
Lies the promise, the heart waits.
A story deep within the soul,
Yearning for the pen's control.

Words may falter, thoughts may stray,
Yet hope persists in its own way.
Through stormy nights and endless days,
The unwritten seeks the sun's warm rays.

For in the blank, potential swells,
A tapestry no one repels.
Resilience blooms, the poem will start,
When courage lifts the timid heart.

The Dance of Color and Chaos

In the swirl of reds and blues,
Chaos twirls in vibrant hues.
Whispers echo through the night,
A dance of shadows, blaze and light.

Beneath the surface, colors blend,
Silent secrets they defend.
Each stroke of fate, a wild chance,
Invoking joy in every glance.

With every pulse, the colors beat,
Racing hearts that skip in heat.
Tangled dreams in neon's glow,
In this chaos, beauty flows.

Amidst the chaos, peace does rise,
In the dance, we find our ties.
Color wraps us, bold and free,
A symphony of you and me.

Fragmented Reflections

Shattered pieces on the floor,
Each a tale, an untold lore.
Reflections warped in glassy sheen,
What was lost, what could have been.

In the silence, echoes ring,
Fragments of a broken spring.
Time unveils the hidden truth,
In chaos lies the youth's own proof.

Mirrored shards, a soul's release,
Through the fragments, we find peace.
Each cut sharp, yet they reveal,
The beauty found in wounds we heal.

As we gather what remains,
New reflections break the chains.
From the past, we weave our thread,
In the light of dreams we tread.

The Heart's Palette

A brush dipped in love's warm hue,
Each stroke a whisper, soft and true.
On canvas bright, emotions flow,
The heart's palette, a vibrant show.

Colors of longing, deep and wide,
In every shade, our fears reside.
Yet in the blend, hope finds a way,
To light the dark and guide the day.

From sorrow's gray to joy's bright gold,
In every tone, a story told.
The heart composes, both wild and free,
An art of life, a symphony.

Each heartbeat paints the world anew,
In the gallery of me and you.
With every hue, our spirits sing,
In love's embrace, we find our spring.

Stories Beneath the Ink

In every line, a tale unfolds,
Whispers of the brave and bold.
Ink upon the page so deep,
Secrets hidden, dreams we keep.

A quill that dances, sharp and keen,
Winds through shadows, sight unseen.
Every letter, a heartbeat's muse,
A narrative, we dare to choose.

Between the words, the real resides,
In silence, truth quietly hides.
A parchment rich with thoughts unspun,
Stories waiting to be won.

So let the ink weave and flow,
In its embrace, our visions grow.
With every scribble, life will spark,
Illuminating the vast dark.

Varnished Hues of Hidden Pain

In shadows cast by silence fell,
A canvas draped in tales to tell.
Colors mixed with tears unshed,
Each stroke a whisper of what's bled.

Beneath the surface, secrets lie,
A palette stained with every sigh.
Varnished layers, brittle thin,
Reflect the battles fought within.

Fragmented hues of fleeting grace,
Emotions trapped in a quiet space.
A beauty born from hurt's embrace,
Each brush a moment, hard to trace.

Yet in the depths, a light does gleam,
A hope that dances in the dream.
Behind the pain, the colors sway,
Varnished hues that fade away.

The Enigma in Every Stroke

Each brush whispers tales unspoken,
A riddle's core, in silence broken.
Lines entwined in a timeless dance,
An enigma wrapped in chance.

Curved edges hold a secret grace,
Where chaos finds a tender space.
With every stroke, a mystery blooms,
In vibrant hues, life's rhythm resumes.

Layers thick with whispers of doubt,
A journey marked with a hidden route.
Colors clash, yet softly blend,
An intricate puzzle without end.

In every shade, a truth concealed,
An artist's heart, forever revealed.
The enigma in each crafted line,
A world untold, both harsh and fine.

Frayed Edges of Forgotten Joys

Faded pages reflect the years,
Frayed edges worn from laughter and tears.
Joy once vibrant, now bittersweet,
Memories linger where shadows meet.

Lost melodies in empty rooms,
Ghosts of happiness, silent blooms.
Each thread unraveled tells a tale,
Of moments cherished, love set sail.

Glimmers of light dance on the brink,
A tapestry woven with threads that shrink.
Frayed edges whisper of yesterday,
Yet beckon us to find our way.

Though time may fade the colors bright,
In the heart, they shimmer with light.
Frayed edges hold the joys we claimed,
In quiet corners, forever named.

Sorrow's Outline in Vivid Shades

In somber tones, the outlines creep,
A portrait drawn from tears we weep.
Vivid shades of sorrow's call,
Each stroke a testament to fall.

The palette holds a heavy hue,
Of heartache stitched with threads of blue.
Yet in the dark, a spark ignites,
Creating beauty from the frights.

Outlined in grief, the shapes do form,
Transforming pain into a storm.
With every shade, a story binds,
In vivid strokes, the heart unwinds.

Sorrow's embrace, a bittersweet song,
In every canvas, we belong.
The outlines tell of lives betrayed,
Yet in their depths, new colors played.

Silence Cast in Color

In shadows deep, the colors fade,
Whispers echo, memories glade.
Brushstrokes blend, a quiet spark,
Silence paints in the cool, dark.

Faded hues of joy and pain,
Life's canvas wears a soft refrain.
Each stroke tells a tale, unique,
Color drips where hearts now speak.

Amid the quiet, colors bleed,
Silence holds what hearts may need.
In stillness, creation blooms bright,
Glimmers of hope ignite the night.

As the palette shifts and sways,
Silent stories light the ways.
In every shade, a world unfolds,
Silence cast in colors bold.

Love's Fleeting Footprints

Footprints linger on the shore,
Soft impressions, evermore.
In the sand, a tale unfolds,
Of whispered dreams and secret holds.

As waves crash in a rhythmic dance,
Love's essence swirls, a fleeting chance.
Each step echoes through the night,
A gentle warmth, a soft light.

With every tide, they come and go,
Memories etched, forever flow.
Yet in the absence, love remains,
A timeless spark through joy and pains.

In shadows cast by setting sun,
Fleeting moments, hearts are one.
Love's footprints fade but never cease,
In every parting, there's release.

Merging Stories in a Chaos of Lines

In a tangle of ink, hearts collide,
Stories merging, worlds inside.
Each line a thread, tightly spun,
Chaos forms where dreams are begun.

Between the verses, echoes play,
Fates entwined in twisted sway.
From every mark, a life escapes,
In whispered tales and shifting shapes.

Time dances through the written word,
Voices mingle, softly heard.
The chaos sings, a vibrant tune,
As stories meet beneath the moon.

In overlapping pages, hearts unite,
A tapestry woven with pure light.
In chaos, beauty finds its way,
Merging truths in disarray.

The Torn Canvas of Adventure

A canvas torn, with colors bright,
Each rip reveals a hidden sight.
Winds of change blow wild and free,
Adventure calls, come dance with me.

Brush in hand, we paint the skies,
Bold strokes form where courage lies.
In every tear, a journey's start,
The torn threads weave through our heart.

Mountains rise and rivers flow,
With each adventure, spirits grow.
Chaos spins in vibrant hues,
Life's adventure, ours to choose.

So fear not the breaks, embrace the thrill,
In torn canvases, dreams fulfill.
With every leap, every fall,
Adventure whispers, heed the call.

Ink's Unquiet Conversations

A scribble of thoughts, a dance on the page,
Whispers of dreams from a quiet sage.
Each word a sigh, each line a plea,
Ink flows like rivers, wild and free.

In shadows it lurks, a fractious beast,
A dialogue rich, from turmoil released.
Confessional lines bleeden truth,
Unfolding the heart, revealing youth.

With every stroke, a soul laid bare,
Conversations sparked in the cool night air.
Ink spills secrets, shadows and light,
Crafting a canvas of truth and fright.

Yet still it calls, this unquiet voice,
In the silence of night, we find our choice.
Writing our stories, with every breath,
Ink's subtle power, a dance with death.

The Journey of an Unseen Heart

In the stillness, a pulse beats slow,
An unseen heart where shadows flow.
Every whisper of hope, a fragile thread,
Mapping a path to where dreams are led.

Through valleys deep and mountains high,
A search for peace beneath the sky.
With hidden scars and untold pain,
The journey winds, a gentle strain.

Fingers trace the lines of fate,
Each heartbeat whispers, it's not too late.
In the silence, a symphony plays,
An unseen heart in a world ablaze.

So we wander, questing for light,
Seeking solace in the darkest night.
The journey continues, both wild and free,
For the unseen heart longs to be.

Sketches of the Soul's Yearning

With a brush of longing, colors collide,
Sketches emerge where dreams reside.
Each stroke a prayer, a silent call,
Yearning for freedom, to rise, to fall.

In the canvas of night, a vision breaks,
Hopes intertwine with heart's mistakes.
Whispers of wishes in shades of gray,
Sketching the soul in a vivid display.

The palette of passions, a bright array,
Capturing moments that slip away.
With every hue, a story told,
Sketches of yearning, bold and gold.

In every corner, desire's spark,
Lighting the shadows, igniting the dark.
The soul's artwork, forever in flight,
Sketches revealing deep inner light.

The Veiled Truth in Color

Colors cascade from a palette unseen,
Veils of truth in shades of serene.
Beneath the surface, lies a tale,
A spectrum of feelings, both vibrant and pale.

Brushstrokes dance, a whispering vibe,
Each hue concealing what words can't describe.
The heart, a canvas, with colors bright,
Hiding the anguish behind the light.

In the layers of paint, emotions blend,
Creating a vision where lies can mend.
Truth is a prism, reflecting the real,
A tapestry woven with every feel.

So stand before this painted art,
And seek the truth that strums the heart.
In the veiled colors, the secrets reside,
A beauty profound that cannot hide.

Milton Keynes UK
Ingram Content Group UK Ltd.
UKHW022116251124
451529UK00012B/545